Contents

Where Goblins Dwell

There is a place where goblins dwell,
where leprechauns abound,
where evil trolls inhabit holes,
and elves are often found,
where unicorns grow silver horns,
and mummies leave their tombs,
where fiery hosts of ashen ghosts
cavort in draughty rooms.

There is a place where poltergeists
and ogres rove unseen,
where witches rise through midnight skies,
where stalks the phantom queen,
where fairy folk atop an oak
are apt to weave a spell;
it's there to find within your mind,
that place where goblins dwell.

Jack Prelutsky

4

John Foster and Korky Paul

Oxford University Press

Oxford   New York   Toronto

Acknowledgements

The editor and publisher are grateful to the following for permission to publish their poems for the first time in this collection:

Andrew Collett, 'The Moon's Magic', Copyright © Andrew Collett 1997.

Paul Cookson, 'Willy the Wizard's Shopping Trip', Copyright © Paul Cookson 1997.

David Harmer, 'Harry Hobgoblin's Superstore' and 'Sir Guy and the Enchanted Princess', Copyright © David Harmer 1997.

Trevor Millum, 'Genie', Copyright © Trevor Millum 1997.

Tony Mitton, 'Dreaming the Unicorn', Copyright © A. R. Mitton 1997.

Michaela Morgan, 'Dinner on Elm Street', Copyright © Michaela Morgan 1997.

Jack Ousbey, 'Quickspell the Wizard', Copyright © Jack Ousbey 1997.

Gareth Owen, 'The Magician', Copyright © Gareth Owen 1997.

Marian Swinger, 'The Lonely Enchanter', Copyright © Marian Swinger 1997.

Charles Thomson, 'A Very Modern Witch', Copyright © Charles Thomson 1997.

Jennifer Tweedie, 'Mang, Katong, and the Crocodile King', Copyright © Jennifer Tweedie 1997.

We also acknowledge permission to include previously published poems:

Richard Edwards, 'Maxo, the Magician', Copyright © Richard Edwards 1993, from *Leopards on Mars* (Viking), and 'The Marvellous Trousers', Copyright © Richard Edwards 1987, from *Whispers from a Wardrobe* (Puffin), both reprinted by permission of Felicity Bryan.

Max Fatchen, 'The Ballad of the Waterbed' from *A Paddock of Poems* by Max Fatchen (Omnibus/Puffin, 1987) Copyright © Max Fatchen 1987, reprinted by permission of the author and John Johnson, Ltd.

Shelagh McGee, 'WANTED — A Witch's Cat' from *Smile Please* (Robson Books, 1976), reprinted by permission of the publishers.

Doug MacLeod, 'Miranda, the Queen of the Air' from *The Fed Up Family Album*, reprinted by permission of the publishers, Penguin Books Australia Ltd.

Jack Prelutsky, 'Where Goblins Dwell' from *The Random Book of Poetry for Children*, Copyright © 1983 by Jack Prelutsky, reprinted by permission of Random House, Inc.

For Georgia Bozas K.P.

Oxford University Press, Great Clarendon Street, Oxford OX2 6DP

Oxford   New York
Athens   Auckland   Bangkok   Bogota   Bombay
Buenos Aires   Calcutta   Cape Town   Dar es Salaam   Delhi
Florence   Hong Kong   Istanbul   Karachi
Kuala Lumpur   Madras   Madrid   Melbourne
Mexico City   Nairobi   Paris   Singapore
Taipei   Tokyo   Toronto

and associated companies in
Berlin   Ibadan

Oxford is a trademark of Oxford University Press

This selection and arrangement © John Foster 1997
Illustrations copyright © Korky Paul 1997

The author and artist have asserted their moral rights to be known as the author and artist of this work.

A CIP catalogue record for this book is available from the British Library

ISBN 0 19 276152 8 (hardback)
ISBN 0 19 276153 6 (paperback)

Printed in Belgium

Quickspell the Wizard

Quickspell the Wizard, whose fame was immense,
Lived deep in the Forests of Knurld,
Across mountains and oceans his spells and his potions
Were known as the best in the world.

His kaftan and kerchief, his tunic and cone-hat
Were a dazzling sight to behold;
The colours of night, plus polar-bear white
With splashes of scarlet and gold.

But one day this wizard stopped paying attention,
His work was haphazard, slap-dash;
His potion went wrong, it was heated too long
And it blew him away in a flash.

Then wizards appeared from far and from near
From Boinka and Ormoc and Flix,
From Komrat and Rhino, from Pinetop and Yorco
They zoomed in to bury the bits.

On horses with wings, on gliders and things
By carpet and hot-air balloon;
And a wizard called Knockit came in on a rocket,
Returning, by chance, from the moon.

With trombones and tubas, with big drums and cymbals
The band played a song of lament;
The coffin was borne by the Wizards of Zorn
Who were ancient and wizened and bent.

By the side of the grave in the afternoon haze
Stood the priest with his book and his bell,
When a voice from the back said, 'My name is Zak
And I've something important to tell.

My master was Quickspell and some time ago
He worked out a potion unique,
When, if any disaster blew up the Old Master
The spell could be spelled, so to speak.'

And then from his doublet he drew out a goblet
And filled it with potions so rare,
On the cry, 'ZIPPERZODED', the mixture exploded
And a great swirl of snow filled the air.

The wizards all watching, half-blinded and blasted
Were bamboozled, amazed, and aghast
When out of the blizzard stepped Quickspell the Wizard
Restored by the spell Zak had cast.

Then the tubas and tambours, the trombones and oboes
Struck up with a song of delight;
A great fire was built on the side of a hill
And the feasting went on all the night.

Quickspell the Wizard and Zak his apprentice
Still live in the Forests of Knurld;
Across mountains and oceans their spells and their potions
Are known as the best in the world.

Jack Ousbey

Harry Hobgoblin's Superstore

You want a gryphon's feather
Or a spell to change the weather?
A pixilating potion
To help you fly an ocean?
Some special brew of magic
To supercharge your broomstick?
Witches, wizards, why not pop
Into Harry's one-stop shop?

Tins of powdered dragon's teeth,
Bottled beetles, newts.
Freeze-dried cobwebs, cats and rats,
Screaming mandrake roots.
Lizard skins stirred widdershins,
A giant's big toe nail,
Second-hand spells used only once
New ones that cannot fail.
Spells to grow some donkey's ears
On the teacher no one likes,
Spells to make you good at sums,
Spells to find lost bikes.

Spells that grow and stretch and shrink,
Spells that make your best friend stink,
Sacks of spells stacked on my shelves,
Come on in, see for yourselves.
Magical prices, tricks galore
At Harry Hobgoblin's Superstore.

David Harmer

Willy the Wizard's Shopping Trip

On Saturday, Willy the Wizard
went into town to do his weekly shopping.

He bought vanishing cream from Roots the Alchemist,
a star-spangled cape from Sparks and Mensa,
a new box of tricks from Ploys 'R' Us,
and twenty-four tins of bats' blood soup
from the supermarket — Asda Cadabra!

Then, he met his friend Don Dracula
for a bite at the Burper King,
before picking up a new cauldron
from 'Voodoo It All — The Druid Yourself Store'.

Paul Cookson

9

Dinner on Elm Street

Thrice the old school cat hath spewed,
Teachers shriek and children whine,
Ring the bell! 'Tis time! 'Tis time!

Round about the cauldron go,
In the mouldy cabbage throw,
Stone-cold custard, thick with lumps,
Germs from Kevin (sick with mumps),
Boil up sprouts for greenish smell,
Add sweaty sock, cheese pie as well.

Froth and splutter, boil and bubble.
March them in here at the double.

Fillet of an ancient steak
In the cauldron boil and bake.
Eye of spud and spawn of frog,
A chocolate moose, a heated dog.
Add the goo from 'twixt the toes
And crusty bits from round the nose.

Froth and splutter, boil and bubble.
March them in here at the double.

Lumpy mincemeat, grey and gristly,
Giblets, gizzards, all things grizzly.
Beak of chicken in a nugget,
With greasy chips the kids will love it.
Scab of knee sprinkle in,
Squeeze juice of pimple from a chin.
Here's the spell to make you thinner,
It's the nightmare Elm Street dinner.

Froth and splutter, boil and bubble.
March them in here at the double!

Michaela Morgan

11

A Very Modern Witch

I'm a very modern witch
(aged about 300 years)
and I've bought a brand-new broom
with a horn and ninety gears.

I leap into the seat
and turn the laser-key:
the acceleration causes
a thrust of several G.

For mine's the only model
where they have introduced
an extra power source
for triple turbo-boost,

so I can fly from London
to New York or Hong Kong —
and back — before the sound
has faded from a gong.

The engine also has
a system that is new
so that instead of octane
it takes my own home brew,

(you know the sort of thing —
dead earwigs, mandrake root,
eggs, hemlock, curried eels,
flat beer and half a boot).

I'm a very modern witch
(aged about 300 years)
and I've bought a brand-new broom
with a horn and ninety gears.

Charles Thomson

The Ballad of the Waterbed

I'll tell you a tale, a spanking yarn
And one to turn your head . . .
Of a boy's delight, how he sailed each night
On his wonderful waterbed.

A waterbed is a magical thing
But not for the timid soul.
It will plunge and lift as the dreamers drift
While the bedroom billows roll.

So he sailed away to a sandy cay
To the pirates' savage lair
Where the gun-lined hulls flew their cross-boned skulls
And gunsmoke filled the air.

He set his sheets for the plundering fleets
Where the victims screamed and bled
And the captains paled, for none outsailed
That scurvy waterbed.

Fierce Captain Kidd had dipped his lid
And Blackbeard cried, 'It's daft,
I've never seen, in the Caribbean,
The likes of this 'ere craft.'

With a swig of rum for his parrot chum
How Long John Silver roared.
But he quickly sank from a salt-stained plank
When he tried to climb aboard.

So the boy came back when the tide grew slack
To the morning clear and bright,
As he woke he said to the waterbed,
'We sail again tonight.'

So woe to the landlubbers left behind . . .
No treasure or diamond rings
But high and dry with a jealous sigh
On their dull old innersprings.

But I'll tell you this . . . where the bow waves hiss
When the midnight's stroke has gone
Don't risk your neck on a waterbed deck
And keep your lifebelt on!

Max Fatchen

The Marvellous Trousers

Last week on my way to a friend's birthday tea
I found them draped over the branch of a tree,
Oh, the Marvellous Trousers.

One leg was striped silver, the other striped blue;
I put them on, closed my eyes, wished and then flew!
Oh, the Marvellous Trousers.

They carried me up like a rocket, so fast
I ruffled the tail of each pigeon I passed,
Oh, the Marvellous Trousers.

I soared over Sicily, rolled over Rome,
And circled the Eiffel Tower on my way home,
Oh, the Marvellous Trousers.

I landed with ribbons of cloud in my hair,
But when I looked down at my legs — they were bare!
Oh, no Marvellous Trousers.

I know it sounds funny, I know it sounds weird,
But somehow and somewhere they'd just disappeared,
Oh, the Marvellous Trousers.

And when I explained at my friend's birthday tea,
The guests shook their heads and blew raspberries at me,
Oh, the Marvellous Trousers.

But I don't care tuppence: I've rolled over Rome,
I've circled the Eiffel Tower on my way home,
I've worn the Marvellous Trousers,
The Marvellous, Marvellous Trousers!

Richard Edwards

16

The Magician

The magician at Daphne's party
Was called The Great Zobezank
But everyone knew he was Daphne's dad
Who worked at the Westminster Bank.

He waved for silence and asked us all
'If there's a volunteer
Who'll step inside my magic box
I'll make you disappear.'

We shouted, 'Mister, please choose me!'
And waved our arms like mad
But he chose Daphne Smart of course
Because he was her dad.

He closed his eyes and raised his wand
And waved it in the air
And when he opened the magic box
Daphne wasn't there.

He bowed and smiled while Daphne's mum
Clapped and we all cheered
Then he uttered the magical words that would make
Daphne re-appear.

But alas when he opened that magic door
No Daphne stood inside
And her father's face turned grey as stone
While her mother wailed and cried.

They called, 'Oh, Daphne please come back!'
And beat upon the door
And as for us we clapped and cheered
Louder than before.

Gareth Owen

Maxo, the Magician

Maxo, the magician,
Was very sharp and slick,
And people flocked from miles around
To see his famous trick,
The one that conjured rabbits,
A hare, two ducks, a cat,
A dozen hens, three foxes
And a goat out of a hat.

Everyone loved Maxo,
They'd 'Bravo!' and applaud,
Yes, everyone loved Max, except
The hat, the hat was bored
And envious — it never got
A single cheer or clap,
And one night at the Hippodrome,
It felt its patience snap.

Maxo, the magician,
Had flashed his brilliant grin,
Had tapped the hat-brim with his wand,
Had started reaching in,
When something startling happened —
He screeched out in alarm,
His hand went in the hat, his wrist,
His elbow, his whole arm,

His cloaked-in-velvet shoulder,
And then, as people cheered,
His head, his chest, his legs and feet
Entirely disappeared.
The audience roared 'Maxo!
Oh, Maxo, sharp and slick,
He's made his whole self vanish
In the hat. Oh, what a trick!'

The curtain fell. The stage-hands
Searched everywhere in vain,
But Maxo, the magician,
Was never seen again.
His dressing-room stands silent now,
And dust lies in his hat,
Which sometimes makes a low
Digestive rumble. Fancy that!

Richard Edwards

Miranda, the Queen of the Air

My Aunty Miranda, a mystic by trade,
Was born in the circus and that's where she stayed.
The people would flock to see Aunty Miranda
Perform with her partner, a Pekingese panda.

'THE QUEEN OF THE AIR' she was fittingly named.
'HER ACT IS UNIQUE!' all the posters exclaimed.
'The Mystic Miranda who comes from the East
Performs levitation on LARGE CHINESE BEASTS!!'

My Aunty Miranda would silence the crowd
And whisper a spell while the panda bear bowed.
Then, after the strange incantation was said
The panda would levitate over her head.

One evening, Miranda misquoted the spell
And there is a plaque where the tragedy fell:
'BELOW LIES MIRANDA, QUEEN OF THE AIR
(Deposed by a plummeting panda bear).'

Doug MacLeod

WANTED—A Witch's Cat

Wanted — a witch's cat.
Must have vigour and spite,
Be expert at hissing,
And good in a fight,
And have balance and poise
On a broomstick at night.

Wanted — a witch's cat.
Must have hypnotic eyes
To tantalize victims
And mesmerize spies,
And be an adept
At scanning the skies.

Wanted — a witch's cat,
With a sly, cunning smile,
A knowledge of spells
And a good deal of guile,
With a fairly hot temper
And plenty of bile.

Wanted — a witch's cat,
Who's not afraid to fly,
For a cat with strong nerves
The salary's high.
Wanted — a witch's cat;
Only the best need apply.

Shelagh McGee

21

Genie

Up in granny's attic, full of ancient junk:
Albums and gramophones and an old wooden trunk.
Peering in the dark — ouch! — ker-clunk!

Tripped over something and hurt my shin
Bruised my leg on this lamp of tin
Then . . . heard a whistling from within!

'Excuse the crutch and the leg in plaster;
What do you desire from me, O master?'

    Oh, no. Just my luck to get
        the Genie of the Magic Lamp.

I banged my head against the wall:
Stars, flashing lights — I saw them all
And heard a deep and magical call:

'Forgive the bandage and the swollen head;
How can I help?' the Genie said.

    Oh no. This time I've got
        the Genie of the Magic Lump.

So . . . I rubbed the lamp with special care
'Genie, Genie, come out of there!'
A whoosh and a whizz and a puff of air!

'I'm the Genie of the Magic Lamp,' I heard it say.
'At last,' I said. 'A proper Genie's come my way.
What shall I do to make it stay?'

'A Genie of wisdom, a sage from afar,
Please speak to me, whoever you are!'
But
When it finally spoke, it just said 'Baa!'

Baa?
    Oh no, I think perhaps I misheard the name
        I've got the Genie of the Magic Lamb!

Trevor Millum

Sir Guy and the Enchanted Princess

Through howling winds on a storm-tossed moor
Sir Guy came to a castle door.

He was led by some strange power
To the deepest dungeon of a ruined tower.

A Princess sat on a jewelled throne
Her lovely features carved in stone.

His body trembled, was she dead?
Then her sweet voice filled his head.

'These evil spirits guard me well,
Brave Sir Knight, please break their spell.

Though I am stone, you shall see,
Kiss me once, I shall be free.'

As demons howled she came to life
Blushed and whispered, 'Have you a wife?'

'My love,' he said, 'still remains
With collecting stamps and spotting trains.

But as long as you do as you're told,
I think you'll do, come on it's cold.'

'Oh,' she cried, 'you weedy bore
I wish I was entranced once more.'

Lightning struck, the demons hissed,
Sir Guy was stone, a voice croaked, 'Missed!'

The Princess rode his horse away
And poor Sir Guy's still there today.

David Harmer

Mang, Katong, and the Crocodile King

Deep in the jungle,
in the land of Mangoree,
lived Mang, the magic drummer,
in a frangipani tree.
Boom-kiri, boom-kiri, boom-boom-kiree.

A boy called Katong
from the village, came to sing,
'Mang, make your magic
melt the Crocodile King.'
Boom-kiri, boom-kiri, boom-boom-karing.

'The Crocodile King
has eaten my ma,
chewed up my gran
and swallowed my pa.'
Boom-kiri, boom-kiri, boom-boom-karaa.

'You are small,' said Mang,
'but you want a great thing.
It will be hard to melt
the Crocodile King.'
Boom-kiri, boom-kiri, boom-boom-karing.

'I will help,' said Katong.
And he beat on the drum
while Mang made his magic,
'Basoko, bagum.'
Boom-kiri, boom-kiri, boom-boom-katum.

Then sparks flew up
from their beating hands
and went whizzing and sizzling
all over the land,
like fireworks made
from the sun and moon,
until they lit up King Croc
in the village lagoon.
Boom-kiri, boom-kiri, boom-boom-boom.

The villagers cheered,
'Hooray! hooray!'
as they saw the sparks melt
King Crocodile away.
Boom-kiri, boom-kiri, boom-boom-kiray.

'He's gone,' cried Katong.
'Now my village is free!'
And Mang said, 'Katong,
come and live with me.
We'll both make magic
in my frangipani tree,
deep in the jungle
in the land of Mangoree.'
Boom-kiri, boom-kiri, boom-boom-karee.

Jennifer Tweedie

Dreaming the Unicorn

I dreamed I saw the Unicorn
last night.
It rippled through the forest,
pearly white,
breathing a moonlit silence.

Its single horn
stood shining like a lance.
I saw it toss its head
and snort and prance
and paw the midnight air.
Its mane was like a mass
of silver hair.

But suddenly it shuddered.
It sensed my spellbound gaze,
my wondering eyes,
and turned to look upon me with surprise,
seeming to read my face
and looking as if to say,
'You are not from this place.
What is your business here?'

My mind was far from clear.
I could not think or speak.
Above my head, I heard the branches creak
and then, from where I stood,
I watched it flicker off into the wood,
into the velvet space between the trees.

A sudden rush of rapid midnight breeze,
that felt both chill and deep,
awoke me from my sleep,
and there upon the pillow by my head
I found a strand of shining silver thread.

I kept that strand of mane,
I keep it, still,
inside a box upon my window sill.
And when the world hangs heavy
on my brain,
it helps me dream the Unicorn again.

Tony Mitton

28

The Moon's Magic

When the moon fell in the ocean
stretching long and wide,
sailing ships all came to see
its magic deep inside.

They came to see its mountains
to touch its secret stone,
but most of all they came to catch
its magic for their own.

They came with giant hammers
to crack its magic face,
they came with ropes and fishing nets
to tie it into place.

They came with swords and daggers
to tear the moon apart,
they came with iron bars
to break its silver heart.

30

They filled their ships with plenty
they piled its magic light,
until the moon, stretching wide,
vanished in the night.

And as they clapped and cheered
for a job they'd done so well,
they disappeared, like magic,
into a midnight spell.

So if you ever notice
the moon long and wide,
walk up close, catch a glimpse
of its magic deep inside.

But before you stop to wonder
for a magic of your own,
watch the moon sinking low
with its sailing ships of stone.

Andrew Collett

31

The Lonely Enchanter

Alone, the enchanter stands,
tall, dark and grim.
His servants, the peasants,
are frightened of him.
He watches the world
from his great castle tower.
Enchantments and magic
have given him power.
They've given him treasure
and wealth without end.
'All this,' he says sadly,
'but never a friend.'

Marian Swinger

32

bushy tail

short ears

Eating nut

Making notes

Once you've spotted some wildlife, use a notebook to write down or sketch some details about them. That way, if they're disturbed and fly or scurry away, then you have some details written down to help you identify them. You could add these to a scrapbook of your nature discoveries to make your own identification book of wildlife in your local area.

Scientific names

Each species has its own scientific name. This name is the same around the world. Many also have their own common name, such as Blackbird or Daisy. The common name might be different in each country, or even within the same country. In Britain, for example, Rowan trees are also called Mountain Ash trees.

5

Hedgehog

Size: 16–25 cm
Scientific name: *Erinaceus europaeus*
Habitat: Hedgerows, parks and gardens
Food: Beetles, worms and slugs
Lifespan: up to 5 years

Hedgehogs have light-brown
tipped spikes on their round bodies.
An adult hedgehog will have between 5–7,000
spines. They are mostly nocturnal, meaning that you will
usually only see them at night. In about October, when the
weather starts to turn colder, hedgehogs hibernate. They dig a
small hole and cover themselves with leaves, either under hedges,
in gardens or in woodland. They come out when the weather gets a
bit warmer again around April.

Urban
Wildlife

A Photographic Guide

Victoria Munson

First published in 2019 by Wayland
Copyright © Hodder and Stoughton, 2019

Wayland, an imprint of
Hachette Children's Group
Part of Hodder and Stoughton
Carmelite House
50 Victoria Embankment
London EC4Y 0DZ
An Hachette UK Company
www.hachette.co.uk
www.hachettechildrens.co.uk

Editor: Victoria Brooker
Designer: Elaine Wilkinson

ISBN: 978 1 5263 1212 9 (hbk)
ISBN: 978 1 5263 1213 6 (pbk)

Printed in China

Acknowledgements:
Shutterstock images: cover: Rudmer Zwerver
(bat), aaltair (mallard), Emi (squirrel), Ian Thraves
Photography (fox), Dom J (road); Title page;
6 Oligo; 8, 10 CreativeNature.nl; 9 Sandy
Hedgepeth; 13 hadot 760; 14 karloss; 15
BeppeNob; 16, 17Martin Fowler; 18 Tompet;
20 Lostry7; 34 Volker Rauch; 34 inset Ziablik;
24 Ralf Neumann; 25 Daniel Prude; 26 Gl0ck;
27 Digoarpi; 28 inset berries Mageon; 29 Andy
Rowland; 29 inset Martin Fowler; 30 LensTravel;
31 Sergey Uryadnikov; 32 top Rob Kemp; 32
bottom craigbirdphotos; 33 bottom Bogdan Boev;
34, 35 IbajaUsap; 36 Rob Kemp; 37 top Martin
Fowler; 37 bottom Martin Spurny; 38 top Ainars
Aunins; 38bAnatoliy Lukich; 39t Gucio_25; 39b
pixel; 40 Peter Zijlstra; 41 Larsek; 42t Grant
Glendinning; 42 Bjorn Stefanson; 43 Vitaly Ilyasov;
48 Kletr; 49 EMJAY SMITH; 50 Brian Maudsley;
51 Arto Hakola; 52 Sue Robinson; 53 Bildagentur
Zoonar GmbH; 54 Mirvav; 55 Adam Edwards;
56 Hannu Rama; 57 artconcept; 58 alslutsky; 59
Florian Andronache; Istock: AntiMartina 19; 40
Bluefly06; 23 RelaxFoto.de; 28 mtreasure; 33 top
Andrew Howe; 44 Derek Audette; 45 Iliuta Goean;
46 Roberto Zocchi; 47t &b rekemp;
Corbis Dietmar Nill/Foto Natura/Minden Pictures/
Corbis 7; Stephen Dalton/Minden Pictures/Corbis
11; Derek Middleton/FLPA/Minden Pictures/
Corbis 12;

Contents

Be an urban nature detective!

To be a nature detective, you need to be observant, patient and quiet. Animals and insects scare easily and can by shy, so it might take time before you can spot them. Some animals are nocturnal, which means they are active at night.

Spotting urban wildlife

You can see urban wildlife in villages, towns and cities. There is wildlife everywhere, from the plants growing in pavement cracks to trees in a churchyard and the insects buzzing past your head. You can be a nature detective in lots of different places, such as in your local park, alongside canals and rivers, or even just walking down the street. Look up, down and around and you'll be amazed at what you can see.

Colour pencils

Binoculars

Notebook

Waterproof jacket

These items might be useful when you're out and about spotting nature.

Large, pointed ears

Fox

Size: 1–1.2 m
Scientific name: *Vulpes vulpes*
Habitat: Towns, woodland and farmland
Food: Mammals, birds and insects
Lifespan: 2–3 years in the wild

Foxes have pointed ears and the same body shape as a dog. They have reddy-orange fur with a bushy, white-tipped tail. Foxes are brilliant hunters, able to sprint and jump. They live in dens hollowed out under a tree root, or sometimes they will live in badger setts. Foxes bury any food they don't eat to come back to later.

Grey Squirrel

Size: 27 cm
Scientific name: *Sciurus carolinensis*
Habitat: Parks, gardens and woodland
Food: Seeds, acorns and nuts
Lifespan: 3–6 years

Large, bushy tail

Long claws

Grey Squirrels were introduced to
Britain from North America in the nineteeth
century and they are now Britain's most common
squirrel. Squirrels are well known for burying food to eat
later. Some food stores are dug up again after a few hours, while
some are found a few months later. Grey Squirrels have very good
memories and use landmarks and smell to find their stores again.

Common Shrew

Size: 7.5 cm
Scientific name: *Sorex araneus*
Habitat: Hedgerows, meadows, marshes and woodland
Food: Insects, slugs, snails and worms
Lifespan: 2 years

The Common Shrew needs to eat every 2–3 hours.

As its name suggests, the Common Shrew is fairly common. It is recognisable by its long, narrow nose. The fur is silky brown and grey on the underside. Common Shrews are always on the move, looking for food. Listen out and sometimes you might hear their high-pitched squeaks.

Large, round
ears

House Mouse

Size: 8–10 cm
Scientific name: *Mus musculus*
Habitat: Farmland and towns
Food: Cereals, seeds, vegetables
and fruit
Lifespan: 1–2 years

The House Mouse's grey-brown
fur and large ears makes it distinct
from other mice. House mice live near
humans and will eat crops and leftover food.
They are good climbers, jumpers and swimmers,
using their tail for balance. They are mostly nocturnal.

Dark grey
fur

Brown Rat

Size: 22–27 cm
Scientific name: *Rattus norvegicus*
Habitat: Urban areas
Food: Scraps of food
Lifespan: up to 18 months

Rats have coarse brown
or dark grey fur, with lighter
coloured underparts and a thick, scaly
tail. They live in colonies in tunnels near
houses and eat food they find lying around.
Rats often groom each other and sleep together
in groups.

Common Pipistrelle Bat

Wingspan: 20–23 cm
Scientific name: *Pipistrellus pipistrellus*
Habitat: Woodland, farmland and towns
Food: Insects
Lifespan: up to 16 years

One Pipistrelle Bat will eat up to 3,000 insects in one night.

These are the most common British bats
and they are also the smallest. They have dark-brown
to rusty coloured fur on their back, and yellowish-brown
fur on their underside. Their nose and ears are black. At dusk,
they come out of their roost, in lofts and buildings, to find food.
If you see one flying, it will have a jerky flight pattern. From mid-November
to April, they hibernate in building crevices, bat boxes, trees and cellars.

Common Daisy

Scientific name: *Bellis perennis*
Height: 4–12 cm
Family: Daisy
Habitat: Fields, meadows and gardens
Flowers: March to October

Daisies got their name from the words 'day's eye' because they close at night and open in the daytime.

Daisies can be seen covering gardens and playing fields from early springtime. The thin, white petals can sometimes be tinged with pink. A large number of tiny florets crowd together to make the bright yellow button in the centre.

Dandelion

Scientific name: *Taraxacum officinale*
Height: 5–40 cm
Family: Daisy
Habitat: Fields, roadsides and grassy places
Flowers: March to October

Dandelion leaves can be eaten in salads or used to make wine and tea.

Dandelions are familiar plants with their heads of bright yellow florets. In late summer, the florets develop into 'dandelion clocks'. These are clusters of small, singled-seeded fruits, each with a tuft of white hairs at the tip. The hairs spread the seeds in the wind like a parachute.

Meadow Buttercup

Scientific name: *Ranunculus acris*
Height: up to 1 m
Family: Buttercup
Habitat: Gardens, fields and meadows
Flowers: May to September

Meadow Buttercups are one of the tallest types of buttercup. They are recognisable by their five bright-yellow, shiny petals and their long, upright stem, surrounded by whorls of thin, pointed green leaves. They have smooth, round stalks.

White Clover

Scientific name: *Trifolium repens*
Height: up to 30 cm
Family: Pea
Habitat: Gardens, fields and meadows
Flowers: May to October

This very common low-growing plant is often found growing near to daisies, buttercups and dandelions. Clover has clusters of tiny white, or pinkish, flowers on thin, upright stalks. The leaves have three round leaflets, marked with a pale 'v' shape.

Stinging Nettle

Scientific name: *Urtica dioica*
Height: 30–150 cm
Family: Nettle
Habitat: Gardens and fields
Flowers: June to September

These common weeds are well-known to all. The dark green, heart-shaped, toothed leaves can give a nasty sting, as can the sharp hairs on the stem. However, they don't sting insects and many butterflies, such as the Peacock and the Red Admiral, lay eggs on them. The hatched caterpillars then eat the nettle leaves.

Cooked nettles can be added to soups, stews and tea.

White Deadnettle

Scientific name: *Lamium album*
Height: 20–60 cm
Family: Mint
Habitat: Hedges, roadsides and waste ground
Flowers: May to December

White Deadnettles look very
similar to Stinging Nettles, but
unlike Stinging Nettles, they don't sting and are
recognisable by the creamy white flowers at the top of
square stems. The flowers have an unusual curved hood
and a lip. Heart-shaped, toothed leaves are covered in fine hair.
Red Deadnettle looks the same as White Deadnettle but have
purplish-pink flowers.

Field Bindweed

Latin name: *Convolvulus arvensis*
Height: 20–75 cm
Family: Bindweed
Habitat: Fields, gardens and waste ground
Flowers: June to September

This pretty flower is in fact a pest because it has long roots that are hard to get rid of. The roots can stretch up to 2 metres underground. Its thin, twisty stem wraps itself tightly around other plants for support. Flowers can be pale pink, white, or pink and white-striped and they smell sweet. Leaves are grey-green, pointed ovals.

Common Mallow

Scientific name: *Malva sylvestris*
Height: 45–90 cm
Family: Mallow
Habitat: Roadsides and grassy areas
Flowers: June to October

Common Mallow have notched, pink petals with dark purple veins. The strong, thick stalk is hairy. Leaves are large and dark green with five lobes. The leaves look crinkly when the plant is young. Mallow can survive without water for a long time.

The ancient Romans used to grow Mallow for food and medicine.

Cow Parsley

Scientific name: *Anthriscus sylvestris*
Height: 60–100 cm
Family: Carrot
Habitat: Hedgerows, fields, roadside verges
Flowers: April to June

Cow Parsley is called 'Queen Anne's lace' after its frilly leaves.

These tall plants have clusters of white flowers on flat flower heads. Many branches of flower heads come from one tall stem, resembling the spokes of an umbrella. The leaves are finely divided into many pairs of toothed leaflets, so they look rather fern-like.

Horse Chestnut

Scientific name: *Aesculus hippocastanum*
Height: up to 40 metres
Life span: up to 300 years

These large trees are better-known as 'conker trees'. In summer, Horse Chestnuts are covered in large spikes of white, or pale pink, flowers. The spiny fruits that grow in autumn contain seeds called conkers. Each leaf is made up of 5–7 long leaflets. The greyish-green bark has large flakes breaking from it. Horse Chestnuts are not edible.

London Plane

Scientific name: *Platanus x hispanica*
Height: up to 35 metres
Life span: up to 500 years

seed balls

Most often found in towns and cities, London Plane trees are said to make up half of the trees in London. They have large glossy leaves about 10 cm wide, with noticeable veins. As the trunk grows, its grey bark continually flakes off revealing a creamy yellow and light brown bark beneath. Through winter, you can see dried brown seed balls hanging from the branches. Seeds are released from these in spring.

Silver Birch

Scientific name: *Betula pendula*
Height: up to 30 metres
Life span: 80–150 years

catkins

Silver Birch gets its name from its
silver-coloured trunk. The bark peels off
in strips leaving dark marks. Heart-shaped leaves
have toothed edges. Male catkins droop downwards and
are about 3 cm long. Female catkins are smaller and upright.

Common Lime

Scientific name: *Tilia x europaea*
Height: up to 40 metres
Life span: up to 400 years

The Common Lime has broad, heart-shaped leaves with toothed edges. You can usually find small tufts of creamy white hair in the leaf veins. Limes attract greenfly and blackfly that feed on the leaves making them sticky. Sweet-smelling, yellow-white flowers appear in July and turn into small seed balls. Suckers grow from the base of the tree.

Small Leaved Lime

Scientific name: *Tilia cordata*
Height: up to 30 metres
Life span: over 500 years

Small Leaved Limes are
often planted in residential
areas, because of their sweet-smelling
flowers. The flowers are white-yellow and hang
in clusters on a long stalk. Fruits are oval with pointed
tips. The hairless leaves are heart-shaped, with a pointed
tip at the end.

Large Leaved Lime

Scientific name: *Tilia platyphyllos*
Height: up to 35 metres
Life span: over 1,000 years

This tall tree has, as its name suggests, larger leaves than the Small Leaved Lime. The leaves have a hairy stalk and the bark is dark brown. Fruits are rounded and smooth with pointed tips. This Lime doesn't produce suckers from the base of the tree.

Hawthorn

Scientific name: *Crataegus monogyna*
Height: 5–12 metres
Life span: up to 250 years

Hawthorn can grow as a shrub, hedge or small tree. The stems of a young hawthorn are covered in sharp thorns. The bark is brown and often covered in green algae. Its leaves are small and deeply-lobed. White flowers appear in spring. In autumn, the flowers turn into dark red berries called 'haws'. These can be used in jams and jellies.

Yew

Scientific name: *Taxus baccata*
Height: up to 30 metres
Life span: over 1,000 years

Yew trees are often found in graveyards. They have a distinctive red flaky bark. The leaves are needle-like, long and narrow. In spring, seeds sit in a bright-red, fleshy cup.

Yew leaves and berries are extremely poisonous to humans.

Holly

Scientific name: *Ilex aquifolium*
Height: up to 25 metres
Life span: up to 300 years

Evergreen Holly trees have tough, spiky leaves. The spikes are to stop animals from eating them. Its bark is silver-grey. In spring, Holly has small, four-petalled, white flowers. Bright red berries in autumn attract many birds.

Bright orange beak

Blackbird

Size: 25 cm
Scientific name: *Turdus merula*
Family: Thrushes
Habitat: Gardens and woodland
Food: Insects, fruit and berries
Life span: up to 5 years

Blackbirds like to eat berries and fruit. Try leaving out old or fallen apples to attract them to your garden.

Male Blackbirds are black with a bright yellowy-orange beak and yellow rings around their eyes. Females and their young are dark brown with a speckled throat. They feed on worms and can be seen hopping across gardens. Look out for them singing loudly from the top of a high perch. The male Blackbird has a beautiful song. It sings all through the breeding season.

House Sparrow

Size: 14–15 cm
Scientific name: *Passer domesticus*
Family: Sparrows
Habitat: Towns and cities, farms
Food: Seeds, scraps and insects
Life span: 2–5 years

The House Sparrow is one of the most familiar small birds in Britain. The male has a grey crown, underside and rump, and a black bib. Its brown back is streaked with black and it has a white bar on its wings. The female House Sparrow is much plainer than the male, without the black markings.

Robin

Size: 14 cm
Scientific name: *Erithacus rubecula*
Family: Chats and thrushes
Habitat: Parks, gardens, woodland and hedgerows
Food: Worms, seeds, fruit and insects
Life span: 3–5 years

Robins are easily recognised by their orange-red breast, brown back and rounded shape. Males and females look alike. Their young have a dark brown, speckled plumage. Robins sing all year round.

In winter, Robins puff up their feathers to keep warm.

Song Thrush

Size: 22 cm
Scientific name: *Turdus philomelos*
Family: Thrushes
Habitat: Parks, gardens, woodland
and hedgerows
Food: Worms, slugs, insects, fruit and berries
Life span: up to 5 years

The Song Thrush is pale brown with a cream-coloured breast
flecked with dark-brown spots. It is slightly smaller than a Blackbird.
When it is in flight, you can see its wings are slightly orange underneath.
Its spots are heart-shaped.

Mistle Thrush

Size: 27 cm
Scientific name: *Turdus viscivorus*
Family: Thrushes
Habitat: Parks, gardens,
woodland and hedgerows
Food: Worms, slugs, insects, fruit and berries
Life span: 5–10 years

The Mistle Thrush is bigger than both the Song Thrush and
the Blackbird. You can tell the two thrushes apart because Mistle Thrushes
are bigger and they do not have the orange colouring beneath their wings.
Their spots are wider and more defined than a Song Thrush's.

Watch for flocks in July and August.

Great Tit

Size: 14 cm
Scientific name: *Parus major*
Family: Tits
Habitat: Gardens, woodland and fields
Food: Insects, seeds and nuts
Life span: 2–3 years

Great Tits
have a clutch
of 5–11 eggs in
April or May.

The Great Tit is the largest
member of the tit family. It has a
distinctive black stripe down its yellow
breast and a glossy black head. Great Tits are
common visitors to bird tables and garden feeders.

Blue cap

Blue Tit

Size: 11.5 cm
Scientific name: *Cyanistes caeruleus*
Family: Tits
Habitat: Gardens, parks and woodland
Food: Insects, caterpillars, seeds and nuts
Life span: 2–3 years

Yellow
breast

Blue Tits are very
colourful, lively birds.
They have a yellow breast
with blue wings and a blue cap.
A pair of Blue Tits can collect hundreds
of caterpillars each day to feed their young.
By the time Blue Tit chicks fly the nest, they
may have eaten up to 10,000 caterpillars.

Collared Dove

Size: 31–33 cm
Scientific name: *Streptopelia decaocto*
Family: Pigeons and doves
Habitat: Gardens and parks
Food: Seeds and grain
Life span: up to 10 years

Black collar

Collared Doves
are recognisable
because of the black 'collar' on
their neck and their pinkish plumage.
They have deep red eyes and reddish feet.
Listen for their 'coo-COO-coo' call.

Collared Doves are not very good nest makers. Sometimes chicks fall through the branches of the nest.

White patch

Woodpigeon

Size: 41 cm
Scientific name: *Columba palumbus*
Family: Pigeons and doves
Habitat: Fields, parks and gardens
Food: Crops, buds, shoots, berries, seeds and nuts.
Life span: up to 10 years

Woodpigeons are the largest and most common of our pigeons. They are grey and have white bars on their wings, which are easier to see when the pigeon is flying. They also have white patches on the sides of their neck. In winter, they can often be found in huge flocks.

Green neck

Feral Pigeon

Size: 32 cm
Scientific name: *Columba livia*
Family: Pigeons and doves
Habitat: Parks and gardens, fields, woodland,
Food: Seeds and cereals
Life span: up to 10 years

This common city bird comes in many different shades, from black to white, grey or brown. They usually have a green or purple sheen on their neck and black wing bars.

Carrion Crow

Size: 46 cm
Scientific name: *Corvus corone*
Family: Crows
Habitat: Parks, roadsides and woodland
Food: Carrion, insects, worms, seeds, fruit and scraps
Life span: 5–10 years

Carrion Crows are usually seen alone or in pairs. They are completely black with a powerful beak. They are intelligent, adaptable and can live almost anywhere. Carrion Crows hop rather than walk.

Magpie

Size: 46 cm
Scientific name: *Pica pica*
Family: Crows
Habitat: Gardens and parks
Food: Insects, plants, carrion, small birds and eggs
Life span: 10–15 years

Magpies are as big as Crows,
but have distinctive black and white plumage.
Up close you can see a green gloss on the tail. They are usually seen in pairs but sometimes flock together in groups of 20–40 to nest.

Black cap

Jackdaw

Size: 33–34 cm
Scientific name: *Corvus monedula*
Family: Crows
Habitat: Parks, gardens, fields, and woodland,
Food: Insects, seeds and scraps
Life span: 5–10 years

The Jackdaw is the smallest crow commonly seen in Britain. It looks black all over, but has a grey neck and cheeks. During the winter, Jackdaws often join Rooks to make large flocks. They have a distinctive 'jack jack' call.

Rook

Size: 44–46 cm
Scientific name: *Corvus frugilegus*
Family: Crows
Habitat: Farmland and woodland
Food: Worms, grains and insects
Life span: 5–10 years

Rooks are slightly smaller than the Carrion Crow and look like they're wearing 'baggy trousers'. You usually see Rooks in large flocks and they nest in colonies (rookeries) at the top of tall trees.

Starling

Size: 21 cm
Scientific name: *Sturnus vulgaris*
Family: Starlings
Habitat: Towns and cities, farms
Food: Insects and fruit
Life span: up to 5 years

Purple-green
sheen on wing

Short tail

Starlings are one of
Britain's most common
garden birds. A Starling looks
black from a distance, but up close
it has a green or purple sheen on its wing.
Starlings live in large flocks and can be very
noisy when grouped together.

40

Ring-necked Parakeet

Size: 39–43 cm
Scientific name: *Psittacula krameri*
Family: Parrots
Habitat: Parks and gardens
Food: Fruit, berries, nuts and seeds
Life span: 20–30 years

Red hooked bill

Long tail

This type of Parakeet escaped from collections near London and bred in the wild. They can now be found across the south-east of England. They are unmistakable with their green bodies, long tails and red bills. Parakeets often form large flocks and can be very noisy!

Chaffinch

Size: 15 cm
Scientific name: *Fringilla coelebs*
Family: Finches
Habitat: Parks, gardens, woodland and hedgerows
Food: Insects and seeds
Life span: 2–5 years

Female Chaffinch

Male Chaffinch

Listen out for Chaffinches singing in early spring.

The male Chaffinch is one of Britain's most colourful birds. Males have a pinky face and breast and a blue-grey crown. Females are sandy brown. Both male and female Chaffinches have black and white wings, and a green rump. During the winter, Chaffinches often group together in large flocks on the edges of woodland, where they search for seeds to eat.

Greenfinch

Size: 15 cm
Scientific name: *Carduelis chloris*
Family: Finches
Habitat: Parks and gardens
Food: Seeds, berries and insects
Life span: 2–3 years

Yellow on wing

The Greenfinch is a popular garden visitor. The male Greenfinch's plumage is mostly yellow and green with bits of grey. Its forked tail has a dark tip. Females can get confused for sparrows, but when they fly off you'll see a flicker of yellow in their tail and wings.

Common Gull

Size: 55–60 cm
Scientific name: *Larus canus*
Family: Gulls
Habitat: Towns and parks, coasts and marshes,
Food: Fish, carrion and insects
Life span: Up to 10 years

Common Gulls have grey
wings, a black tail with white
bars, a white head and body, and a
yellow beak. In winter (pictured) their
white head is specked with grey.

Mute Swan

Size: 140–160 cm
Scientific name: *Cygnus olor*
Family: Swans, ducks and geese
Habitat: Rivers, ponds and lakes
Food: Water plants, insects and snails
Life span: 15–20 years

Young swans are called cygnets.

Mute Swans are Britain's largest bird. They are white with a long 's'-shaped neck and an orange bill with a black tip. They have a lump at the top of their beak. Swans can get angry and will hiss and flap their wings. A male swan is called a 'cob'; a female is called a 'pen'.

45

Mallard

Size: 50–65 cm
Scientific name: *Anas platyrhynchos*
Family: Swans, ducks and geese
Habitat: Ponds, rivers and lakes
Food: Seeds, acorns and berries,
    plants, insects and shellfish.
Life span: 15–25 years

Mallards have a clutch of 9–13 eggs.

Female

Male

The Mallard is the most
common type of duck in Britain.
The male Mallard has a green head,
a white ring around its neck, a brown
breast and a pale grey back. The female
Mallard is speckled brown.

46

Moorhen

Size: 32–35 cm
Scientific name: *Gallinula chloropus*
Family: Swans, ducks and geese
Habitat: Ponds, rivers and lakes
Food: Water plants, seeds, fruit, grasses, insects, snails, worms and small fish
Life span: up to 15 years

Moorhens are black, with a red forehead and a yellow-tipped red beak. They have long green toes and white along their wings and tail.

Coot

Size: 36–38 cm
Scientific name: *Fulica atra*
Family: Rails
Habitat: Ponds, rivers and lakes
Food: Vegetation, snails and insect larvae
Life span: up to 15 years

Coots and Moorhens can often be seen together, but Coots are slightly larger and have a white forehead and beak.

Coots can run along the surface of water.

Honey Bee

Scientific name: *Apis mellifera*
Size: 1.6 cm
Habitat: Gardens, parks, woodland

Honey Bees have slightly hairy, brown-black bodies with orangey-yellow bands and large black eyes. They will sting when they feel threatened, but once they have stung they die, unlike Common Wasps who can sting again and again. Honey Bees live together in large numbers in nests.

48

Red-tailed Bumblebee

Scientific name: *Bombus lapidarius*
Size: 2.3 cm
Habitat: Gardens, farmland, woodland and hedgerows

Red-tailed Bumblebees are very common bumblebees. The females are large black bees with a red tail. Males are smaller than females and have two yellow bands on the thorax and one at the base of the abdomen. They build nests in walls, in straw in stables, or in abandoned birds' nests. Look for them feeding on daisies, dandelions and thistles.

Seven-spot Ladybird

Scientific name: *Coccinella 7-punctata*
Size: up to 6 mm
Habitat: Gardens, parks and woodland

Ladybirds can beat their wings 85 times per second

This small, round beetle has bright-red wing cases dotted with seven black spots. The bright colour warns predators that it tastes horrible. If a ladybird thinks it is about to be attacked, it will produce small blobs of yellow blood from its legs as a warning. In summer, female ladybirds lay clusters of eggs on leaves. The eggs hatch into small black larvae. The larvae have spiky grey-blue skin with yellow spots. The larvae turn into pupae, which become adult ladybirds in a couple of weeks.

Black Garden Ant

Scientific name: *Lasius niger*
Size: up to 0.5 cm
Habitat: Gardens, parks, woodlands

One Black Ant colony can contain more than 5,000 ants.

Black Garden Ants live together in huge colonies on the ground. Worker Black Ants are wingless, brown-black females that cannot breed. Each colony has one or two queen ants that are much larger than worker ants. Male ants are smaller than females and have wings.

Pond Skater

Scientific name: *Gerris lacustris*
Size: 1.5 cm
Habitat: Ponds and lakes

Pond Skaters are small bugs with a brownish-black, narrow body. They have tiny hairs on their feet that repel water and allow them to 'skate' on the surface of ponds. They use their middle pair of legs to move themselves forwards with a rowing or jumping motion, and they use their rear pair of legs to steer left or right. The front pair of legs is used to catch and hold insects to eat.

Crane Fly

Scientific name: *Tipula paludosa*
Size: 2 cm
Habitat: Gardens, parks and grassy areas

Crane Flies have long, grey-brown bodies and long legs, which give them their nickname 'Daddy-Long-Legs'. Their two wings are thin and translucent. Crane Flies are attracted by lights, which is why they often fly into houses in the evening. They sometimes lose a leg trying to escape from a predator, but they can still survive without one or two legs.

Large White

Scientific name: *Pieris brassicae*
Wingspan: 6 cm
Habitat: Gardens, parks and farmland
Family: Whites and yellows

Large Whites are also known as 'Cabbage Whites'

Large White butterflies look very similar to Small Whites, but Large Whites are, as the name gives away, much larger and their black markings are much darker. Females have two black spots while the males have no spots. Caterpillars are grey-green and mottled with black spots and yellow stripes. They stay as pupae through winter and adults emerge in spring. The caterpillars love to feed on cabbages, so they are not popular with farmers.

Small White

Scientific name: *Pieris rapae*
Wingspan: 5 cm
Family: Whites and yellows
Habitat: Gardens, parks and farmland

One of the most common butterflies in Britain, the Small White is, as its name suggests, small and white. The females have two black spots and a black streak on the forewings. Males also have two black spots, but the second of these spots is much lighter. Small White caterpillars are a pest because they like to feed on cabbages and Brussels sprouts.

Peacock

Scientific name: *Inachis io*
Wingspan: 6.5–7.5 cm
Habitat: Gardens, fields and orchards
Family: Nymphalids

Peacock caterpillars like to eat nettles.

This common garden
butterfly has striking yellow and
blue eyespots on the tip of each wing.
These spots give the butterfly its name because
they look like the markings on a peacock bird. In winter,
Peacock butterflies hibernate in hollow trees and sheds.

Red Admiral

Scientific name: *Vanessa atalanta*
Wingspan: 5.5–6 cm
Habitat: most habitats
Family: Nymphalids

These striking red and black butterflies are common visitors to gardens. They have bars of red on their fore and hindwings, with white spots on the tips of their forewings. The underside of their wings is a dark brown and black, which provides good camouflage when they rest on tree bark.

57

Small Tortoiseshell

Scientific name: *Aglais urticae*
Wingspan: 4.5–6.2 cm
Habitat: Woodland, grassland, gardens,
       city centres
Family: Nymphalids

Small Tortoiseshell butterflies
are bright orange with black and
yellow bars on their forewings and black
arches filled with blue edging on all four wings.
Female Tortoiseshells can lay 80–100 eggs on the
underside of nettle leaves.

Common Earwig

Scientific name: *Forficula auricularia*
Size: 1.3–1.8 cm
Habitat: Gardens, parks and woodland

Earwigs got their name because of their ear-shaped wings.

Common Earwigs are easy to identify because they have prominent pincers at the rear end of their body. Male Earwigs have a pair of long curved pincers, while female pincers are smaller and straighter. Both have shiny brown bodies. Although they have wings, it is rare to see Common Earwigs flying. They are mostly nocturnal, coming out at night to feed.

Further information

Places to visit

National Trust
www.nationaltrust.org.uk/visit/places/find-a-place-to-visit

Protecting a range of spaces and places in England, Wales and Northern Ireland, the National Trust takes care of forests, woods, fens, beaches, farmland, moorland and nature reserves as well as historic houses and gardens. Find somewhere new to visit in your local area or further afield.

The Wildlife Trusts
www.wildlifetrusts.org/visit
Find a nature reserve near you

National Wildflower Centre www.nwc.org.uk
The National Wildflower Centre aims to raise awareness of the importance of wildflowers to the environment. It has seasonal displays and encourages people to create their own wildflower areas.

www.rspb.org.uk/reserves
Find out about more than 150 RSPB nature reserves where you can watch wildlife

Useful websites

www.butterfly-conservation.org/679/a-z-of-butterflies.html
The Butterfly Conservation website has an excellent A-Z of butterflies and moths. Find out how to register for the Big Butterfly Count.

www.mammal.org.uk
Information and downloadable factsheets on all British mammals

www.nhm.ac.uk/take-part/identify-nature.html
The Natural History Museum has several identification guides

www.plantlife.org.uk/wild_plants/plant_species/
An A-Z of wild flowers with descriptions and photographs

www.rspb.org.uk
Information on every bird, including a bird identifier. Find out how to register for the Big Garden Birdwatch.

www.wildlifetrusts.org/wildlife/species-explorer
The Wildlife Trusts species explorer page gives you photographs and descriptions of British animals, fish, amphibians and birds

www.woodlandtrust.org.uk/learn/british-trees
Identification guides to native and non-native British trees, including sections on places to visit

Glossary

abdomen the back part of an insect, joined to the thorax

bar a patch of colour on a bird

bark the outside of a tree's trunk

beak the hard mouth part of a bird

belly the part of a bird's body between its breast and its tail

breast the part of a bird's body between its throat and belly

camouflage colours on an animal's body that blend with the background, making it difficult to spot

catkins petalless flowers that hang from trees and are usually pollinated by the wind

clutch a group of eggs laid at one time

colonies groups of the same animal that all live together

crown the top part of a bird's head

family a grouping of species that are similar

flock a group of birds

floret small flowers

flower head a cluster of small flowers that often look like one flower

forewing the front, or forward, wing of an insect

fruit the part of a plant that holds the seeds

habitat the place where a plant or an animal lives in the wild

hibernate to spend winter sleeping

hindwing the back, or backward, wing of an insect

leaflet a small, separate part of a leaf

native an animal, tree or plant that grows naturally in an area

nocturnal active at night

petals the showy part of the flower which attract insects

plumage a bird's feathers

predator an animal that hunts and eats other animals

roost a place where birds or bats rest

rump the area of a bird's body above its tail

species one of the groups into which trees, plants and other living things are divided

suckers a new branch that grows from the base of a tree

thorax the middle part of the body of an insect – the legs and wings are attached to the thorax

translucent partly see-through

whorls rings of leaves around the stem of a plant

Index